AF083920

JaTaKa TaLeS

 ADAPTED FROM THE ORIGINAL AMAR CHITRA KATHA COMICS!

First published in India in 2023 by HarperCollins Children's Books
An imprint of HarperCollins Publishers
4th Floor, Tower A, Building No. 10, Phase II, DLF Cyber City,
Gurugram, Haryana – 122002
www.harpercollins.co.in

6 8 10 9 7 5

Text © Amar Chitra Katha 2023
Illustrations © Amar Chitra Katha 2023

P-ISBN: 978-935-6990-15-9
E-ISBN: 978-935-6990-02-9

This is a work of fiction and all characters and incidents described
in this book are the product of the author's imagination. Any
resemblance to actual persons, living or dead, is entirely coincidental.

Neel Debdutt Paul and Nalini Sorensen assert the moral right to be
identified as the authors of this work.

All rights reserved. No part of this publication may be reproduced,
stored in a retrieval system, or transmitted, in any form or by
any means, electronic, mechanical, photocopying, recording or
otherwise, without the prior permission of the publishers.

Cover and inside illustrations: Based on the artwork in
the original Amar Chitra Katha comics

Typeset in Baloo 13pt/ 16
by Ketan Tondwalkar

Printed and bound at Nutech Print Services - India

This book is printed on FSC® certified paper
which ensures responsible forest management.

JaTaka Tales

Adapted from the original
Amar Chitra Katha comics

WRiTTen By
Neel DeBDuTT Paul and
NaLini Sorensen

Contents

The Monkey King's Sacrifice	7
The Loyal General	29
The Two Kings	44
The Golden Deer	57
Monkey's Heart	78
The Wish Tree	91
True Friendship	106

The Monkey King's Sacrifice

It's hard to imagine, but centuries ago, humans had not yet discovered the wonders of the mango. This magical fruit was kept a secret, deep in a jungle. It was guarded by a troop of monkeys. Their home was around a beautiful old mango tree on the banks of a wide, raging river.

Each spring, the monkeys would look up at the tiny little green fruit when it was in early bloom. They would salivate at the thought of those tiny little buds blossoming into the ripe, sweet and marvellous mangoes that they would enjoy for months to come.

During one such spring, all the monkeys gathered for their weekly council under the shade of the great mango tree. Every one of them was in a good mood at the thought of the tree bearing her beautiful fruit.

However, sulking in the corner was the monkey king, his face clouded in deep thought.

The monkey king had always been jolly, the first to crack a joke, quick to give advice, and always ready to break into song or into his strange, lovely monkey dance. So, that morning, watching their king so reflective, the rest of the troop was alarmed.

"What is it, Sire?" asked one.

"What troubles you?" questioned another.

"Here we are, ready to jump and laugh and celebrate spring, and there you are, sitting in a corner, not saying a word," said a wise, old, troubled monkey. "What's on your mind, Your Majesty?"

The king turned towards his audience. Slowly, he rose.

"There are troubles coming, my dear friends. I can sense them."

"What do you mean?" said the wise one.

"There are dark clouds gathering. I see them across the river."

All the monkeys turned towards the distant bank. They saw nothing.

"What are these riddles you spout? I've had enough of this!" came an impatient voice.

You see, the king was not unchallenged.

His brother, an evil, angry monkey, had always resented the king. He had once wanted the throne, but the wise troop had voted against making him king. His brother had become the leader and this monkey had always held a grudge.

"I will tell you. I fear that men are coming for our beautiful home. I have observed mankind closely all through my life. I think I understand them. If they want something, they will stop at nothing to get it. We all love our precious mangoes, don't we? What prevents them from loving mangoes too? I fear that if man gets hold of even a single mango, he will stop at nothing to get more. We must do everything we can to protect our trees."

"What shall we do?"

"Oh! This is so scary!"

"You mean we will lose our home?"

Loud, fearful cries echoed throughout the gathering.

The king raised his hand.

"Silence. I know what we must do. We cannot let a single mango fall into the river. All of you, quick! Gather all the buds that bloom on those trees with branches over the river. We cannot let any fruit grow there. By no means should the fishermen get hold of these mangoes."

The king's brother was not happy. "If we pick the buds, oh wise king, won't we be left with fewer mangoes later in the year?" he grumbled.

The wise monkey spoke up, "Yes. You are right. But we will still have fruit from the trees elsewhere, and most importantly, we will be saving our home. What would you prefer? A belly full of mangoes for one summer or a home for years to come?"

Soon, each monkey was tasked with a branch

over the river, and they all went to work, carefully picking each bud from their assigned branch.

All except one.

The king's brother was not just evil, he was lazy too.

"Who cares? That fool of a king has a nightmare, and we must all fall in line, emptying our trees," he muttered to himself, as he reluctantly picked the buds off his branch.

He picked a few, but deliberately left a few on the branch.

Weeks passed, and the light breeze of early summer started to blow through the land. The first few mangoes fell to the ground from the trees away from the river, and the monkeys rejoiced. It was mango season! They laughed, danced, ate and celebrated.

But, what the king feared most was about to happen.

Two fishermen had laid their nets early that morning on the river. As they waited in their boat, a beautiful ripe mango ripped from its branch and

PLOP!

— fell right into the net.

That evening, as the fishermen reeled in their nets and counted the fish, they found a strange-looking fruit right in the middle of their catch. Puzzled by this strange object, they decided to take it home with them.

When they reached home, they had no idea what to make of this strange fruit. It smelled wonderful and a part of them wanted to dig in right away. But there was another part that was suspicious – what if it tasted awful? Or worse! What if it was poisonous?

They decided not to risk themselves and to take it to their king instead. He'd know what to do.

As they entered the palace gate, the king's guards stopped them.

"HALT! Who goes there?"

"We are here to show this strange fruit we have found to King Mahasa. We do not know what it is, whether it is poisonous or the best fruit in the land."

"YOU WISH TO POISON OUR KING!" the guards exclaimed angrily.

"No! Sir, the horror! Not at all. We wish to merely show him our discovery. It is for him to decide what to do with it."

"Fine. You may enter. But we have our eyes on you."

The fishermen entered the palace, now shaking with nervousness.

As they approached the king, they looked at each other for support and presented their discovery.

"Our beloved King, Sire, Ruler of our land, waters and fish, we have made a discovery that we wish to present to you," said the first fisherman.

The second fisherman cleared his throat and raised the mango above his bowed head.

"We found this in our nets this morning, Sire. We do not know what it is, but it smells heavenly. We have come all this way to share it with you."

King Mahasa had never seen such a fruit before. He sent for his chief forester immediately.

"What is this, Forester? I have never seen a fruit such as this," he demanded.

"Sire, I have never seen this fruit before either. But, if I am not mistaken, according to the Shastras, it is the mythical mango. I believe it to be the tastiest fruit on earth. For years I have looked for this."

King Mahasa was still suspicious. "Is it poisonous?"

"Not at all," responded the forester. "I believe it is sweet and fragrant. In fact, it is referred to as the king of fruits."

King Mahasa needed no further encouragement. He took a massive bite, unable to wait any longer.

"My goodness! This is the best fruit I have ever tasted. Actually, wait. This might be the best food I have tasted in my life! I want more. Right away. Fishermen, here are two gold coins. Take me to the spot where you set your nets this morning.

Ministers, prepare a party. I want archers, cooks and tents. I may even call upon the bard. We leave now!"

So, King Mahasa along with his party, left on two boats.

As they arrived on the shore, they were greeted by the sight of the beautiful, old mango tree. King Mahasa quickly jumped off the boat, leapt at a mango, plucked it out from the stem and sunk his teeth into its marvellous flesh. He then invited the entire party to follow his lead.

He turned to his minister and said, "We will camp here tonight and possibly for another few days. I cannot resist this fruit. I must have my fill."

"Your wish is my command, Sire!" said the minister obediently.

Tents were pitched, the cooks got to work and King Mahasa sat back, enjoying his fruit, relaxing and listening to the songs of his bard.

As dusk slowly turned into night, King Mahasa was ready to turn in. Suddenly, there was the sound of twigs breaking. Then a few more. Then the screeching of animals.

King Mahasa turned to his minister, concerned. "What is that sound? Are there wild animals here?"

"No, Sire, just monkeys," he said. "There is nothing to worry about."

"Well, have a few killed by the archers in the morning. Tomorrow, we will lunch on mangoes and monkey flesh," the king replied with a wicked glint in his eyes.

The next morning, as the first rays of sunshine hit the mango tree, the monkeys woke up to a barrage of arrows.

"Master! What do we do? We will all die!" they screeched as they ran in panic.

The monkey king had to think fast. "Follow me," he said.

He tied a strong vine from the nearby banyan tree around his waist, pondered the width of the river across from him, and jumped with complete disregard for his own safety.

But, as the monkey king swung across the river, he realized, to his horror, that the vine

was not long enough. He would just about manage to grab hold of a branch on the other shore, but for his fellow monkey tribe to cross over, he would have to be the bridge.

As arrows whizzed past his ears, the monkey king shrieked at his tribe, "CLIMB ACROSS THE VINE NOW! I AM HOLDING ON."

The first monkey crossed the river. She hesitated right at the end. "Master, I have to step on you. How can I, a lowly member of your tribe, step on my king?"

"This is not the time!" ordered the king. "We all have to do what we need to do to survive. Step on my shoulder and jump on to the shore. NOW!"

As a trail of monkeys crossed the river, King Mahasa noticed the brave monkey king holding on for dear life. The sight filled him with a strange thought: "Confronted by the same situation, where my people are in trouble, will I be able to show such bravery?"

He ordered his men to stop shooting at the monkeys.

Most of the monkeys were now safely across to the other side of the river. However, the king was quickly losing his grip and there was just one monkey left to cross. It was his evil brother.

As he crossed, he thought to himself, "This is a golden opportunity! I can get rid of this so-called 'king', and become the leader myself!"

The monkey king shouted at his brother, "Hurry up! I can't hold on much longer."

His brother responded, "Well, you won't have to hold on much longer, dear brother!"

He leapt and landed a sharp kick right on the king's head. The monkey king lost his grip and plummeted to the ground.

King Mahasa watched the scene unfold with horror. He jumped on a boat and rushed to the aid of the fallen monkey king across the river.

"Let me help you, dear friend. I am sorry to have caused all this trouble. Come with me. You have inspired me so very much," he said to the monkey king. The monkey king nodded his head slightly. King Mahasa bowed his head.

"Would you please allow me to take five mangoes from the tree here? Come with me to my kingdom. I will take care of you."

Then he turned to the crowd of monkeys gathered around them. "All of you, come with me. Come to my kingdom. We will grow a great mango orchard in the name of your king. You, and all the generations that follow, may stay in the orchard, protect it, feed from it and live off it. I ask only one thing in return—that you allow me and my people to share this beautiful fruit with you."

The fame of King Mahasa's mango orchard spread like wildfire. Throughout the world, the mango

travelled. Even today, you will find the countryside dotted with beautiful mango orchards ...

... and in many of these orchards, you will still find the monkey king's descendants, stealing a mango here, throwing a seed there.

THE LOYAL GENERAL

The king of Varanasi was loved by all. He was approachable, kept an open mind, and treated everyone with respect. He was always compassionate and fair towards his subjects.

This general feeling of happiness and justice seemed to trickle down to not just all the people, but to every animal and bird in his kingdom too.

The crow king of Varanasi, King Cawashia, was much loved too. Of all the kings the crows had ever had, King Cawashia was the most kind and just.

The crows from the neighbouring kingdoms were more than a little envious of the crows in Varanasi, only because of their king.

He was also a true family man, who dearly loved his wife, Queen Kaualia. He valued her intelligence and opinion. Often, Queen Kaualia joined King Cawashia as he sat in court deciding important matters of the crow kingdom.

One day, as King Cawashia and Queen Kaualia flew past the kitchen window of the palace of the king of Varanasi, Queen Kaualia spotted the fish that the royal chef was cooking for the king. The mere sight of it made her mouth water. She longed to have just a tiny bit of it for herself. It kept her awake at night.

Queen Kaualia was usually a sound sleeper.
"What is it, my love? Why can't you sleep?" asked King Cawashia, truly concerned.

"It's nothing," Queen Kaualia replied.

"It can't be nothing! Why don't you tell me? Don't you know? You are my queen! There is nothing I wouldn't do for you!" declared King Cawashia.

"Well, do you remember we flew past the palace this evening?" asked the queen.

"Go on," said King Cawashia.

"I saw the fish that the royal chef was cooking for the king of Varanasi, as we flew past the kitchen window. And, I know it sounds silly, but I can't seem to get it out of my mind. I think I will die if I can't taste just a bit of it. I don't want the kind of food we eat. I'm longing to taste the fish that's on the king's table!" cawed Queen Kaualia, in a very agitated manner.

King Cawashia was deeply disturbed. This was a problem unlike any other.

He softly cawed and comforted Queen Kaualia, and promised to look into the matter in the morning.

But he didn't sleep well that night. He tossed and turned, wondering how he could possibly solve this problem.

The next morning, as King Cawashia continued to ponder on the problem, his general flew by.

"You seem troubled, Your Majesty. What seems to bother you?" the general asked, bowing low before King Cawashia.

King Cawashia replied, "I seem to have a problem like no other." He proceeded to explain the matter to the general.

The general listened to the king attentively. Then, he smiled.

"Don't worry, Your Majesty. I have a solution. I will see to it that our queen gets the food she craves. Leave it to me. Consider it done," said the general.

With a quick bow, he left King Cawashia.

King Cawashia was relieved. He flew over to Queen Kaualia.

"My love," he said, "The general has promised to take care of your wish. Let's leave it to him. I have faith in him."

Queen Kaualia was extremely pleased. King Cawashia was a bit nervous. He hoped that his general would solve this issue, somehow.

He was, however, relieved and delighted to see a smile back on his queen's face.

Meanwhile, the crow general took eight of his best crow soldiers with him and flew towards the king's palace.

"Attention, Soldiers! We will perch on the royal kitchen roof!" commanded the general.

As they landed on the roof and stood at attention in a neatly spaced line, the general debriefed his soldiers, "Listen carefully. While the royal chef takes the food to the king, I will peck on him till he drops the dishes. As soon as that happens, you must move swiftly. You four must fill your beaks with rice, and you four must fill your beaks with fish. And then, fly as fast as you can back to Queen Kaualia and give it to her. Do you understand?"

"Yes, Sir!" obediently cawed the crow soldiers.

The general solemnly nodded his big, black head. These were his most able soldiers. He had confidence in them.

"Ah! Here comes the royal chef. As soon as he crosses over to the open courtyard, I will strike," said the general, puffing out his chest and taking in a few deep breaths. "Follow my lead now!"

As the royal chef stepped into the courtyard, the crow general swooped down and attacked him. In the blink of an eye, he pecked him on his head, neck and cheek.

The royal chef moved his hand to swat him away. The tray lost its balance. The dishes on it fell to the ground with a loud

C-R-A-S-H!

In all the chaos, the eight crow soldiers swiftly zoomed onto the scene. Four filled their beaks with rice, four filled their beaks with fish, and took flight – exactly as the general had ordered them to.

There was so much noise and uproar that the king came to his window and watched the scene unfold in utter disbelief.

"Don't worry about the dishes! Catch that crow!" yelled the king to the royal guards who had reached the courtyard. The general was just about to fly away, when the royal guard clamped his hands over him. He struggled and wriggled around, pecking wildly, but he couldn't free himself from the royal guard's grasp.

"Good you caught him," yelled the king from the window. "Bring him to me at once!"

As the royal guard took him inside the palace, the general thought to himself, "I'm glad that the queen's longing will be satisfied. They can do anything to me now. I have done my duty towards my king. That's all that matters."

As soon as they reached the king of Varanasi, he demanded, "What was that, Crow? You have

displeased me, and you have risked your very life with this foolish venture. Speak up! What do you have to say for yourself? I do not take kindly to thieves."

The crow general bowed his head low and replied, "Your Majesty, I'm sorry to have displeased you. I am not a thief. The food was not for me. I am the crow general. I did this only for my king, King Cawashia, and for my queen, Queen Kaualia. I will do anything for my king, just as your subjects will do anything for you, Your Majesty." He went on to explain what had happened.

The king of Varanasi was stunned into silence. He said, "I am impressed by your loyalty to your king, general. Such loyalty is rare. It needs to be rewarded."

Turning towards the royal guard, the king commanded, "Set the crow general free! Now!" As the general bowed before the king of Varanasi, the king said, "And henceforth, a portion of all the food cooked for me by the royal chef will be sent every day to King Cawashia, Queen Kaualia and you, general. You won't need to do this again."

"Thank you, Your Majesty," said the general, as he bowed down before him. Then he hopped onto the ledge of the window, spread his wings and flew up into the sky.

THE TWO KINGS

King Mallika was a powerful and just man. He ruled over his kingdom of Kosala with kindness, intelligence and honesty. He was always caring and impartial towards his subjects, who loved him.

However, King Mallika continuously strived to find ways to become a better person and king. He set the bar very high for himself.

Often, he would question his ministers, "Tell me the truth! I demand it! Is there a flaw in my character? How can I get better?"

"No, Your Majesty!"

"No, Sire, no! It's not possible to get better, Sire."

"You are gentle, generous and just, Your Majesty."

King Mallika was not satisfied. He felt that they were not being honest, because he was their king.

So, he set off in his chariot to question the people in his city.

"Tell me, what do you think is my greatest fault?" King Mallika asked a man who was passing by.

"Your Majesty, you have none," replied the man, bowing low. "You are the best king to have ever ruled Kosala, Your Majesty."

"Is there a fault in my character?" King Mallika asked another passerby.

"You rule wisely and well, Your Majesty," came the prompt reply.

"Hmm," said King Mallika to himself. "This cannot possibly be true. I think my ministers and my people are afraid to tell me the truth. They think that I will punish them. Maybe I should go out to the countryside where they won't recognize me so easily, and ask the people there."

So, he got back into his chariot and set off to the countryside. Before long, the roads seemed to get quieter and greener. The birds started singing loudly.

Along the way, King Mallika saw a farmer working in his fields. King Mallika asked his charioteer to stop. He took off his crown, got down from his chariot, and walked across the field to the farmer.

"Hello, my friend! It's a hot day," said King Mallika, trying to begin a conversation.

The farmer stopped working, took out a handkerchief, and wiped the sweat off his forehead. He gave the king a slight nod and sipped some water.

"What are you growing?" asked the king.

"Rice in that part, and vegetables in this one," replied the farmer wearily pointing at the two sides of the field with his index finger.

"Such a shame that King Mallika does not give our farmers more help," said King Mallika tentatively.

"Do NOT speak badly of our king! I will not tolerate it. There is no one as virtuous as our great king, King Mallika. He is the best king that Kosala has ever had! He treats his subjects like his children."

King Mallika was speechless. Deep in thought, he made his way back to his chariot. Even after all this, he couldn't shake off that little kernel of doubt that still remained – maybe his subjects were still lying to him.

He got into his chariot and asked his charioteer to drive him further into the kingdom. As the road curved towards the right, there was a narrow

bridge ahead of them. King Mallika's chariot rolled onto the narrow bridge, the wheels clanging on the wood. From the other end of the bridge, there was another chariot approaching.

In those days, the general practice deemed that the right of way was always given to the person who was superior. The charioteer of King Mallika bent forward and yelled out to the other charioteer, "Halt! Hold your horses!"

The other charioteer shouted right back, "Let no one come in the way of my royal master. I have with me the king of Varanasi."

"And I have with me the king of Kosala," King Mallika's charioteer said right back.

This was truly a strange situation. Both chariots carried kings. Who should move aside and give way to the other?

"Let age or power decide. How old is your master and how large is his kingdom?" asked King

Mallika's charioteer.

"Fifty-five years old, and …"

"Unbelievable!" interrupted King Mallika's charioteer. "My king is also fifty-five years old!"

The strange situation on the bridge continued to build up, with both kings ruling kingdoms of the same size too. In frustration, the king of Varanasi's charioteer suggested, "Let the better man have

the right of way. Agree?"

"Agree. But who IS the better man?" asked King Mallika's charioteer. "My master is the best king that Kosala has ever had. He repays evil with evil and good with good," he continued.

"Aha! If those are your master's virtues, then I shudder to think what his faults are," replied the other charioteer.

"Be quiet!" yelled King Mallika's charioteer.

King Mallika put his arm on his charioteer's shoulder and nodded at him to stop. His heart started racing, but he looked calmly at the other charioteer, and said, "Go on. What did you mean by that?"

"Your Majesty, please accept my apologies," said the charioteer. "I didn't mean to be rude. What I meant was, my master repays even evil with good. He does good no matter what, even to those who harm him. They need good the most is what he says."

There was a long pause as King Mallika reflected on the wisdom of these words.

"Then he is a better man than me. Draw back my chariot. Let the good king of Varanasi proceed before me," said King Mallika, respectfully bowing his head ever so gently as the other chariot went by.

King Mallika now knew what he needed to work on to become a better king and a better person.

THE GOLDEN DEER

Mahadhanaka was the son of a wealthy merchant in Varanasi. His parents gave him nothing but the best. He ate the best food, dressed in the best clothes and didn't work a day in his life.

He inherited a lot of money from his parents, but didn't know how to manage it. He spent his money on any little – or big – thing that caught his fancy.

And, guess what happened? His money ran out. Very soon, Mahadhanaka didn't have a paisa to his name.

Since he hadn't worked a day in his life, Mahadhanaka was confused. He did not know how to get more money. So, Mahadhanaka decided to go and borrow money from a moneylender. He didn't know what else to do.

"Maniramji," said Mahadhanaka, "I need some money. Will you lend me some?"

"How is it possible that you need money, Mahadhanaka?" asked Maniram, raising his eyebrows in disbelief.

"Err … err … I'm looking to start a new business," replied Mahadhanaka.

"Well, because of the goodwill that your parents fostered, I will lend you money. But, it will have to be at the same rate of interest that I offer all the others," said Maniram, ever the cunning businessman.

"Yes, yes. Any rate is okay. I'll return your money as soon as I become rich again," said Mahadhanaka.

Maniram was surprised, but tried not to show it. There was no negotiation! He didn't even ask about the rate of interest!

And so, it started.

Mahadhanaka went from one moneylender to the next in Varanasi. He was delighted at how easy it was for him to accumulate money. But he had put no thought whatsoever into how he would pay the moneylenders back.

Months went by, and when Maniram realized that Mahadhanaka showed no signs of returning his money, he paid him a visit.

"Mahadhanaka, how are you?" asked Maniram.

"As well as anyone can be, Maniramji. Would you like some tea?" replied Mahadhanaka.

"Actually, I'm pressed for time today. But I wanted to come by and meet you and ask when I could get my money and interest back?"

"Err ... err ... Business has not been g-g-g-good," stammered Mahadhanaka.

"I don't want things to get ugly between us," said Maniramji in an ominous tone. "It is owing to my regard for your parents that I am paying you this visit. I need my money back by 6 p.m. on Friday."

And, very soon, every moneylender Mahadhanaka had borrowed from paid him a similar visit. Mahadhanaka knew he had no way of repaying them, as he had not earned even a rupee.

It was only a matter of time before word of Mahadhanaka's debts spread amongst the moneylenders across the city. He had borrowed money from every one of them.

So, they decided to join forces. They paid him a visit together, a big angry mob of moneylenders.

As soon as they laid eyes on him, they shouted, "Give us our money back!"

Poor Mahadhanaka was terrified. He did the only thing he could think of.

He lied.

"Calm down! Calm down! I have a huge treasure hidden in the river bed. Come with me, friends. We will go and get it, and I will return all the money that I have borrowed from each of you. Every last paisa."

As they walked towards the river bed, Mahadhanaka tried to put a plan in place.

In the end, he thought he would jump into the river and swim away, and get as far as possible from the mob of moneylenders. Perhaps he could swim to Gaya and then run away. He was not a strong swimmer, but he hadn't had the chance to think of a better plan. And he was afraid of the angry moneylenders.

Mahadhanaka stopped at the river bed, and said, "Friends, I would like you to wait here. I will jump into the river and swim to the spot where the treasure is hidden. When I signal to you, you should be ready to help me pull out the treasure.

It will be heavy. I will not be able to drag it here by myself."

The moneylenders looked extremely relieved and happy that they would be getting their money soon. With a small wave, Mahadhanaka jumped into the river.

However, things didn't go according to plan. Mahadhanaka had not paid attention during his swimming lessons, and the current in the river was strong. He soon found himself thrashing around in the water, and running out of breath.

"Help! Help!" Mahadhanaka gasped.

But the moneylenders were too far away. The river had turned and twisted, and the moneylenders could neither see nor hear him.

Mahadhanaka started getting frantic. "HELP! HELP!" he screamed.

Not very far from where this was happening, lived Ruru, a golden deer. As he was munching on some grass, he heard Mahadhanaka's cries for help. He ran to the river bank and, without a thought, jumped right into the river. He swam towards Mahadhanaka, and then said urgently, "Grab on to my back!"

He slowly made his way back to the river bank with Mahadhanaka safely with him. Mahadhanaka was very grateful.

"How can I ever thank you? You have saved my life!" said Mahadhanaka, after he had recovered.

"There is only one thing I ask of you. Promise me that you will not tell anyone where I live. A golden deer is a rare sight, and I do not want people to disturb my peace as I live my life."

"Oh absolutely!" said Mahadhanaka. "I promise you."

As luck would have it, that very night, Queen Khema, the queen of Varanasi, dreamt of a golden deer.

She woke her husband and said, "I have dreamt of a golden deer, who will be able to take away all my aches and pains. I have dreamt that this is the only cure for my failing health."

"Don't worry, my dear," replied the king. "If there is such an animal, I will find him."

The next morning, the king sent for his councillors, and wrote a decree for all his subjects.

The town crier went to the centre of the town, rolled out the scroll, and yelled at the top of his lungs –

Here Ye! Hear Ye!

**By royal decree,
Queen Khema has bestowed a task
of great importance upon you,
her royal subjects.**

**You are to report to Queen Khema
on the sighting of a golden deer.**

**A reward of a sack of gold coins
will be given to any royal subject
who can report the whereabouts
of the said deer.**

And, guess who was walking by as this happened? You are right! Mahadhanaka.

"What a coincidence!" whispered Mahadhanaka to himself. And without thinking it through, he ran to the town crier. "Take me to the king or queen IMMEDIATELY! I have information for them about a golden deer," he declared.

The town crier puffed out his chest with importance, and took Mahadhanaka to the palace with him.

He bowed before the king. "Your Majesty, I have someone who has information about a golden deer." The king was extremely pleased to hear this.

"What is your name?" he asked.

"Your Majesty, I am Mahadhanaka," he replied, bowing low. "At the break of dawn, I can lead you to a golden deer who lives on the banks of the river. I have seen him with my own eyes. I can take you to him, and you can capture him."

"This makes me happy. You will stay the night at the palace, and we will leave at dawn tomorrow," declared the king.

They left bright and early the next morning, and Mahadhanaka led them to where the golden deer lived, without taking a single wrong turn.

"There, Your Majesty, can you see that grove of mango and sal trees? The golden deer lives there."

"Surround the grove! And get me that deer! Alive!" commanded the king.

The soldiers did as they were commanded, and in no time at all, Ruru was captured and brought to the king. He was struggling to be freed, till his eyes fell on Mahadhanaka.

"You! I should have known all along it was you!" he yelled angrily. "It would have been better to save a log of wood than a man like you!"

"What do you mean?" asked the king.

"Your Majesty, I saved this man's life. I saved him from drowning and in return all that I asked was that he should not disclose my whereabouts to anyone. This is how he has repaid me."

The king was furious!

"Is this the truth?"

"But ... B-b-b-but ..." Mahadhanaka stammered.

"I've half a mind to sentence you to death!" said the king, his face red with anger.

"No, Your Majesty. Please do not do that. I don't want him to die because of me," pleaded Ruru.

"You are truly a rare deer," said the king. "Ask for anything, and I will grant it. I will not harm you, Ruru. I only need you to visit Queen Khema at the palace, and cure her of her aches and pains."

"Of course, Your Majesty. It would be my pleasure and my honour to help the queen in any way I can. All I ask is that from now on, no animal or bird be harmed by anyone in your kingdom. No one should have to live in fear."

"Absolutely," agreed the king. "I will draft a decree as soon as we are back at the palace."

From that day forth, by royal decree, not a hair or feather of any animal or bird was harmed in the kingdom.

Monkey's Heart

On the banks of a mighty river lived a solitary monkey. He had left his troop years ago and was happy to live off the fruit of the only tree that grew on that particular river bank. He liked to think that for one monkey, one tree was enough.

A little downstream, on another bank, lived a crocodile and his wife. For years, they had ruled over their little strip of the bank, gorging on any animal that dared to venture there. When animals stopped coming, they switched to the fish in the river, the occasional mice that scampered through; and once in a while, if they were lucky, they attacked the boats that the humans rode down the river.

One afternoon, after a particularly long stretch of time without eating any animal meat, the crocodile's wife spoke up.

"Enough!" she said. "I want a monkey's heart. I was dreaming about eating one just last night. If

you don't get me a monkey's heart, I am going to go upstream and find a monkey myself!"

"How do I find a monkey's heart, dear?" responded her husband.

"Well, you're a crocodile, aren't you? You're supposed to be cunning! Go on then, prove that the saying is right. Use your smarts and find me a monkey's heart to eat."

"Sigh!" the crocodile thought. "She's in one of her moods. I'd better get on with it."

So, the crocodile swam upstream. He rested, as still as a rock, in the middle of the river. Just downstream from him, he spotted a monkey – our solitary monkey – leaning against his tree. The crocodile thought of a plan.

A little later, the monkey's afternoon snooze was interrupted.

"Hey! You there! Monkey! Can you hear me?" It was the slimy, nasty crocodile, trying to get the monkey's attention.

"Yes, Crocodile. What do you want?" replied the monkey.

"Say, you can't be happy here all the time. You know the other bank over there," said the crocodile. "The one just downstream from here? It's a lot more fun there."

"Yes. I know that bank. A long time ago, when I was still with my troop, I remember a crocodile just like you had attacked us there."

"Well, I'm not THAT crocodile, Sir! No! No! No! And even if I were, I would've changed my wicked ways. I don't eat monkeys, Sir. Believe me. Come with me, and I will show you the most beautiful river bank."

He paused. Then, he added, "There are fruits of all kinds there! Aren't you tired of eating just one fruit from that one tree you have here?"

"Sigh! You are right, dear Crocodile. I am rather happy here, and I truly love my home, but the same fruit day in and day out, all year round ... sometimes I do wish I had something new and different."

"So ... come! It is right there! Right across the river."

"But there's a problem, Crocodile. I can't swim!" exclaimed the monkey.

"That is not a problem, my dear friend. See, I can swim. Just hop on to my back! I'll take you across," responded the crocodile, trying hard to stop himself from smacking his lips.

Now you see, our monkey was a simple one. He did not have too many needs and he certainly was not greedy. For years he had spent time on his own, making friends with a migratory bird here, who had promptly flown away as soon as it was summer, or a plump fish there, who swam away after a while. Our monkey was lonely. Dazzled by the prospect of making a friend just down the river, the monkey decided to trust the crocodile. He jumped on his back and off they went!

"This is lovely, my friend. Thank you for this!" said the grateful monkey.

"Oh, little do you know, Monkey. I should thank you!" thought the crocodile, with an evil smile, as he started to sink lower and lower into the river.

Suddenly, the monkey found himself waist deep

in the water. Then he was chest deep. And soon, his face was bobbing up and down!

"Hey! Stop! ... GURGLE ... Friend! What are you doing? ... GURGLE ... Are you trying to drown me?"

"Why, of course, you foolish monkey," said the crocodile as he came up to the surface again. "I am going to drown you and then I'm going to eat you. And your heart, Monkey, your heart will be a present for my wife!"

"Oh Lord!" thought the monkey. "What have I got myself into? I must think fast."

So, our monkey thought, and thought fast. He came up with a brilliant plan.

"HAHAHAHAHAHAHA!"

The monkey started laughing at the crocodile.

"What?" asked the crocodile, truly surprised. "Why are you laughing?"

"Don't you know, dear friend? We monkeys hide our hearts in a special, secret place when we are young. You can eat me, dear Crocodile, but you will never ever eat my heart."

"What? Is this true?"

"Indeed, Sir," responded the monkey. "When I was just a little boy, I hid my heart in a secret spot in the tree. But, since you have been so very kind to me, I will make a deal with you."

"What are your terms?" asked the crocodile.

"If you spare my life, I will give you my heart. Don't eat me, and I will let you take my heart to your wife," said the monkey.

"Well, that's very kind, dear Monkey. Those are great terms. Fine. Take me to your heart."

"You will have to turn around and take me back to my home, dear friend," responded the monkey.

Soon, the two were closing in on the bank. The monkey pointed high, to the very top of that solitary tree.

"There. That is where I keep my heart, Sir. Take me back home and I will go and fetch my heart for you," he said.

As soon as they were back on the bank, however, the monkey leapt high, onto the top of the tree, out of the reach of the crocodile, and taunted, "You are such a fool, dear friend! How can I take my heart out? Don't you know that if I took my heart out of my body, I'd be dead? You really thought I had kept my heart in a secret location?"

The crocodile stared at him in complete disbelief. "I thought we were friends!" he said.

That made the monkey pause. "We can't be friends if I have this fear of you eating me, right? You need to win back my trust. Come back often to this bank, and let's see if we can be friends. God knows I could use one."

And that is how, for years to come, passing birds, fish and even humans were confused at this strange sight on the banks of the river – a crocodile on the land below and a monkey, perched on some branches above, at a safe distance, deep in conversation with each other.

THE WISH TREE

There was once a little village on the outskirts of a tiny town. The village was located just off one of the largest roads in the country. Hundreds, if not thousands, of merchants, their bullock carts and travellers went past this village on this large road each day. The men of the village, though, didn't do very much.

You see, just outside the village was a tree. It looked like a mango tree. The fruit that weighed down its branches looked exactly like mangoes. The smell wafted through the air, all around the tree, smelling just like a bounteous mango tree. The villagers called this tree their kalpavriksha or wish tree.

Just to the left of the tree that looked like a mango tree, a few jagged rocks jutted out of the ground, away from the road. Each morning, the men of the village would gather and hide behind these rocks, looking over their beloved tree, waiting for unsuspecting travellers.

Each morning, the smell of the fruit would waft into the nostrils of at least one traveller or merchant, who would not be able to resist the urge to get off the road, find the tree, pluck a fruit, bite into it and ...

THUD!

That morning was no different. As the men peered over the rocks, a merchant walked towards the tree.

"OOOOH! This one looks plump! He'll be rich for sure," said one of the villagers.

"Yes! Look at that gold chain around his neck. Who knows what else he has in those bags of his," said another.

Soon, the merchant reached out for a mango, bit into it and, as if on cue ...

THUD!

The poor man dropped dead. The kalpavriksha, you see, was poisonous. The cruel villagers preyed on these unwitting travellers and robbed them every day. Most of the villagers had stopped doing any work. The craftsman had put his tools away, the potter had let his kiln grow cold, the farmer's field lay dry and barren, and the fisherman's nets lay empty and covered in dust. All the villagers had became thieves. Everyone, to the last man. They had made a small fortune through this treachery.

When they had just started, there were a few of them who had refused to take any part in this horrid venture. There had been a meeting in this village and a few good men had initially stood up to the rotten men who had come up with this idea. You see, this tree had grown for years, but bore fruit much later. On the day it finally bore fruit, the villagers found a monkey stone cold dead at the bottom of the tree.

They soon realized that there was poison in the fruit and forbade all the villagers from eating it. That was when some of the villagers hatched this cruel plan.

"See," they reasoned, "we're not killing anyone. If anything, the tree is. If someone mistakes the fruit for a mango and dies, is it a sin that we take a few of their things? We can even perform their last rites and make sure their souls are taken care of in the afterlife!"

At first, only a few villagers had taken up this cruel business. But soon, word spread of the riches that were to be made in the venture. One by one, all the villagers had joined them and they had all become as rotten as the poison in the fruit of their wish tree.

Days turned into weeks, and then into months. Every villager had made a nice and healthy profit off the poor souls who had fallen victim to the tree.

Then, one day ...

"Look!" cried one of the villagers. "There's a caravan heading this way!"

"I can't believe our luck! There's a merchant for each one of us today, boys!"

The group of villagers were jubilant.

Soon, four merchants broke away from the caravan and made a beeline for the tree.

"I'll climb up," said one. "Let me pluck a few of these mangoes and throw them down. Let's gather enough for everyone!"

One of them climbed the tree and three of them stood below, ready to catch the fruit as he plucked it. The one who had climbed the tree threw down one mango after another, and the three men below gathered them neatly. Soon, they had gathered enough.

"All right, come down now. We can each eat a delicious mango, while we wait for the others to join us."

Before you knew it, they had each taken a bite of the mango. Suddenly ...

"STOP!" a voice yelled across the field. The caravan had arrived and at its head was a wise

merchant. "Those aren't mangoes at all! Those are poisonous fruit! Do not take another bite!"

"But, Sir, we've already eaten some!" cried one of the four men.

"Quick! Have this!" the merchant grabbed a small vial of a green liquid from his pack. "It is an antidote. This will make you vomit out all the poison in your body!"

The villagers who were quietly watching this from behind the rocks were beside themselves.

"How did he know?"

"Is there a mark on the tree?"

"Oh Lord! This is bad for business!"

"We need to know how that merchant knew about the tree. If there is a mark, we must make

sure we erase it so that no other traveller ever finds out."

One of the villagers ventured out from behind the rocks. Soon, the others joined him.

"Kind sirs," he cried. "Did you eat a mango from our poison tree? Are you all right?"

"Yes!" said the wise merchant. "I got here just in time. These gentlemen had taken a bite each, but I had my antidote, and they have now all vomited out the poison. They are safe."

"Oh! Thank god! This dastardly tree!" shouted another villager. "We have been trying to warn travellers about it for so long. How did you know that it was poisonous?"

"It was simple!" replied the wise man. "You see, all fruit-bearing trees near a village are deprived of their fruit by the villagers and their children.

This one was heaving with ripe mangoes and so easy to climb. But not one fruit seemed to be plucked. The only conclusion was that the fruit was poisonous. Now before we go, we shall cut this tree down for you!"

Before they could be stopped, the merchants had brought out their saws. The villagers watched silently as their kalpavriksha was cut down right in front of their eyes.

Soon, the village returned to normal life. The craftsman's tools were back to being busy, the potter's kiln had a raging fire, the farmer's lands gave bounteous crops and the fisherman's nets were heaving with fish.

The poison from their kalpavriksha soon left the village and the men understood that there are no shortcuts to wealth. They may not be rich anymore, but they seemed to be happier. They all went back to working honestly, and the village soon forgot about their rotten wish tree.

TRUE FRIENDSHIP

Just outside a forest near Varanasi, there lived a hunter who was particularly unhappy. He was going through a lean period – he hadn't caught a single animal in weeks. One morning, he woke up grumbling about the usual route he took. He had to shake things up. He would try a new path that morning. So, he set out on an unfamiliar route. Not many hunters went that way and he felt confident that, sooner or later, he would find some prey.

He continued grumbling as he walked all day. As it neared evening, he turned back, and just as he was about to give up, he saw the most amazing sight!

Not far away sat three of the closest friends the forest had ever seen. In a thicket, near a secret lake, sat a tortoise, a woodpecker and an antelope.

"A tortoise challenged a hare to a race home. How did she win?" said the tortoise.

"Oh no! Another tortoise joke? Gah!" said the antelope.

"By going into her shell, of course!" giggled the tortoise, proudly.

"On that note, I am going home!" said the woodpecker.

"Yes, I suppose it is getting late," replied the tortoise.

"Tomorrow morning then, folks? Goodnight!" said the antelope.

"Goodnight!" replied the others as they walked away.

The hunter, meanwhile, crouched behind a bush, salivating.

"That antelope will feed me for days," thought the hunter. He decided to lay a trap and come back

early the next morning. So, he hung up a rope on a low branch of a nearby tree.

"He is bound to come back this way tomorrow. His hoof will get caught in this rope and he will not be able to free himself. I cannot wait. An antelope that big? It will be breakfast, lunch and dinner for months!"

The next morning, at the crack of dawn, the three animals, the antelope, the woodpecker, the tortoise, individually made their way towards the thicket. Around the same time, the hunter too walked that way. The tortoise was thinking about how beautiful the morning was, the woodpecker about how pretty all the trees looked, and the antelope about how nice his life was. But all the hunter could think about was his prey – the antelope – and all the meat that he would soon have!

Just as the antelope turned towards the thicket, he put his foot in the rope, took a step ahead, and the trap hoisted him up. In no time, the poor creature was strung upside down, wailing for his friends.

The tortoise and the woodpecker rushed to the poor antelope.

"Please help me, my friends!" cried the antelope.

"Who could have done this?" asked the tortoise as he saw his friend hanging from the tree. "I thought this was the safest forest in Varanasi."

"I know exactly who," said the woodpecker. "It is that dratted hunter who lives at the forest's edge. I saw him do this to a deer only a few months ago. We need to think fast."

"Okay, but can you guys think a little faster here?" cried the frantic antelope, hanging upside down.

"All right, Tortoise, you have sharp teeth to bite through that rope. Go and fetch the ladder and I will go and buy us some time. I know the hunter must already be on his way."

And so, the tortoise fetched the ladder, climbed up, and started biting on the rope to free his friend.

"I truly thank you for this, dear tortoise, but can you possibly GO A LITTLE FASTER ALREADY?" pleaded the panicking antelope.

"I'm going as fast as I can! I'm just not as fast as you!"

Meanwhile, the hunter heard the cries of the antelope. He rushed out of the door of his hut. The woodpecker spied him, swooped down and gave him one painful, powerful peck on the head.

"OUCH!!!"

"Okay, so now what do I do?" thought the hunter, once he was back in his hut. "I've got it. I'll go through the back door."

Just then, however, the woodpecker was thinking, "Hmm. I wonder what he'll do next. I bet he will try to escape through the back door."

The hunter quietly opened the back door of his hut and looked outside.

"Looks like it's all clear here.

HAHAHAHA!

Fooled you, bird!" he thought.

"Just as I thought," whispered the woodpecker, as he hid right behind the hut.

WHACK!

went the woodpecker. The hunter turned around and rushed back towards his house.

He had forgotten, however, that he had closed the door. He ran straight into his shut front door, and slumped down, unconscious.

Leaving him there, the woodpecker rushed back to the thicket.

"You'd better hurry, Tortoise. I slowed him down, but he's a tough nut to crack. I'm sure he'll be here

soon," said the woodpecker. "There he is! Hurry!"
Just then, the tortoise managed to cut through the
rope and the antelope came crashing down.

THUD!

But, there was no time to rejoice.

The antelope and the woodpecker made a run for
it, but as usual, the tortoise was far too slow. The
hunter soon caught up with him.

"You! You tortoise! You're the one who freed my antelope. I'll teach you to interfere with my hunt," screamed the raging hunter. "Since you robbed me of my dinner, I'll put you in my sack, take you home and eat you. I hear tortoise soup is particularly tasty!"

As the hunter bagged the tortoise, the antelope looked on from behind a bush.

"Oh Lord," he thought. "My poor friend. The hunter has caught him because of me. I must help him. Maybe, if I show myself, the hunter will see me, try to catch me and then my friend can escape."

So, the antelope stepped out from behind the bush gingerly. As soon as he had done so, the greedy hunter spotted him.

"Oh! There's my antelope. Forget this tortoise! I want that antelope!"

He dropped the tortoise and ran towards the antelope.

The antelope thought fast. "I'll lead him to my favourite cave. It is so big and dark. Once he's in there, he will never be able to find his way out!"

The antelope rushed into the mouth of a cave,

closely followed by the hunter. Suddenly, the hunter was completely engulfed in utter darkness! In no time, the antelope had found his way out of the cave, leaving the hunter inside.

"Hey! Where did he go? Where am I? Why is it so dark? How do I get out of here? OH, MY GOD! I AM SO SCARED OF THE DARK! Somebody help me!" screamed the hunter, as the fear in him grew into utter panic.

The antelope rushed to his friend, still in the bag, and freed him.

Soon the woodpecker came down from the tree and joined his friends.

"So, what happened to the hunter?" he asked.

"He's still going around in circles in our cave!" replied the antelope.

The stories in this collection are adapted from the following Amar Chitra Katha comics:

Monkey Stories

THE MONKEY KING'S SACRIFICE
Script: Meena Talim
Art: Jeffrey Fowler

THE MONKEY'S HEART
Script: Meena Talim
Art: Jeffrey Fowler

Deer Stories

RURU, THE GOLDEN DEER
Script: The ACK Editorial Team
Art: Jeffrey Fowler

TRUE FRIENDSHIP
Script: The ACK Editorial Team
Art: Jeffrey Fowler

Bird Stories

THE LOYAL GENERAL
Script: Kamala Chandrakant
Art: Ashok Dongre

Stories of Wisdom

THE TWO KINGS
Script: Luis M Fernandes
Art: Dilip Kadam

THE FRUIT TREE
Script: Luis M Fernandes
Art: Dilip Kadam

THE AMAR CHITRA KATHA CHAPTER BOOK SERIES

India's rich tapestry is woven together by her stories. These tales can be from the great epics and mythology, or from the ancient history of this rich land. But sometimes the stories of the people, passed down from generation to generation – told at bedtimes and celebrations, in schools and homes – are the most astounding. These are the stories that are part of the great collective inheritance from our past generations.

The Amar Chitra Katha chapter book series brings together some of the greatest tales in the Amar Chitra Katha catalogue. These stories are a celebration of the great collective inheritance from our past generations and aim to bring the reader closer to the thoughts and traditions that make up our country's identity.

The first set in the series, Amar Chitra Katha Folktales Collection, includes *Buddhist Stories*, *Tales of Wit and Wisdom* and *Funny Folktales*.

The second set in the series, Timeless Classics From Amar Chitra Katha, includes *Amazing Folktales*, *Fascinating Stories* and *Unusual Fables*.

The third set in the series, Most Loved Amar Chitra Katha Stories, includes *Jataka Tales*, *Fabulous Fables from India* and *Witty Minister Stories*.

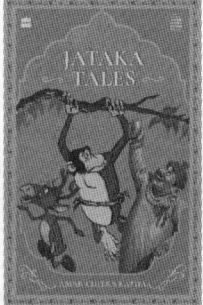

ABOUT ACK

Amar Chitra Katha was founded in 1967 and is a household name in India. It is synonymous with the visual reinvention of the quintessentially Indian stories from the great epics, mythology, history, literature, oral folktales and many other sources.

With a heavy bent on authenticity and meticulous research, Amar Chitra Katha prides itself on being the most informative and trusted storyteller for children. The stories in this series have been adapted directly from the comics for young readers.

Today, Amar Chitra Katha is a cultural phenomenon, custodian of more than 400 comics in 20+ languages that have sold 100+ million copies to date. Amar Chitra Katha is available in bookstores, online and across digital platforms.